Garden
Haiku

Other book by Lily Wang, M.A.

Baby Haiku
Turn Your Parenting Experience into an Empowering Journey!

Introduction

A newborn's arrival in the world can be a frustrating and challenging time for new parents. Trying to understand a baby's wants and needs is often complex, leaving parents exhausted and looking for answers.

Lily Wang has the solution with *Baby Haiku*, an innovative and powerful book of haiku poetry perfect for the time-starved new parents. Combining the essence of Eastern and Western poetics, Wang creates an essential tool to help you understand your baby through the simplicity of haiku.

Wang skillfully revives the role of poetry to delight and instruct. "The true motivation behind this book," Wang said, "is to make a better tomorrow for future generations by honoring what parents are doing today."

Most parents are physically and materially ready for a baby's arrival. But mental preparation is sometimes more difficult to obtain. Wang helps bridge this gap with her inspirational poems that speak deeply to a parent's soul. Parents will learn how to relax and enjoy this special time, achieving a Zen-like existence in their chaotic lives.

Wang helps parents experience the true sense of significance associated with taking care of a baby. With *Baby Haiku*, parenthood becomes an empowering spiritual journey!

ISBN: 0-595-37687-8   6 x 9   Trade Paper   60 pages $9.95
ISBN: 0-595-82069-7   6 x 9   Adobe ebook   60 pages $6.00

Author and poet, Lily Wang speaks at libraries and book clubs. Seminars include a lecture, popular question/answer session, and autographing. Please visit her website, www.lilywang.org for details.

What Reviewers Are Saying about *Baby Haiku*

"Upwards of 80% of all new mothers experience some degree of postpartum depression. By taking a few moments to read through the 52, three line formatted, haiku poems comprising Lilly Wang's very highly recommended "Baby Haiku" poetry collection, any new mother experiencing the 'baby blues' can find comfort and therapeutic reflection. The poetry is thoroughly 'reader friendly', contemporary, and focused upon having a new baby, celebrating the bonding of a mother to her child, and applying an Asian style wisdom to a commonly encountered and contemporary experience. #28 Pray for one more grace/To share his kindred soul--/A pink blossom, it's a girl.

—Midwest Book Review

"Verses on parent- and babyhood, penned by a mother. Throughout, Wang illustrates parenting at its most desirable, capturing all the wonder of a baby's transformation into a child. These are appealing, bite-size vignettes just right for new parents."

—Kirkus Reviews

"The family is one of the greatest blessings one can experience in life. Strong families build first-rate communities. Thank you for your contribution to families through your poetry."

—Nathan Magsig, mayor of Clovis, CA

"The haiku structure doesn't inhibit Lily Wang from creating beautiful images filled with love, wonder, emotions, and transcendental spirituality. This is a beautiful book of memories that anyone will cherish."

—Krista Riggs, Fresno County librarian

"This is beautiful and moving poetry. The reviewer is a mother and can relate very strongly to the emotion and depth of the poetry. The author uses sensory imagery, as well as poetic devices such as metaphor and simile to convey meaning. The author does an extremely good job of conveying feeling and theme in such a few short lines."

—iUniverse editor

"I felt this had a powerful message for not only new moms but for all of us. We are connected by birth and growth, and we all experience this miracle in one form or another. I enjoyed the haiku form with everyday language yet elevated with figurative devices. In our busy lives, shorter but meaningful messages are essential."

—Jill Lane, founder of WBW Book Club

"*Baby Haiku* is a perfect combination of Eastern subtlety and Western sense of humor. Each poem of haiku, though no more than three lines, is a picture of a thousand words. Babies sometimes may be playful and practical. They are always delightful. Wang reminds us every baby is a treasure worth exploring."

—Yung Cheng, principal of Hwa Sha College

Garden Haiku

RAISING YOUR CHILD WITH ANCIENT WISDOM

Lily Wang
Author of *Baby Haiku:*
3-Line Poems for New Parents

iUniverse, Inc.
New York Lincoln Shanghai

Garden Haiku
Raising Your Child with Ancient Wisdom

iUniverse books may be ordered through booksellers or by contacting:

iUniverse
2021 Pine Lake Road, Suite 100
Lincoln, NE 68512
www.iuniverse.com
1-800-Authors (1-800-288-4677)

Because of the dynamic nature of the Internet, any Web addresses or links contained in this book may have changed since publication and may no longer be valid.

The views expressed in this work are solely those of the author and do not necessarily reflect the views of the publisher, and the publisher hereby disclaims any responsibility for them.

ISBN: 978-0-595-43095-6 (pbk)
ISBN: 978-0-595-87435-4 (ebk)

Printed in the United States of America

This book is dedicated to all parents and to my husband, Haidar, a wonderful gardener and engineer

Contents

II. Messages for Children

III. Haiku on My Children and Family

IV. Nature/Season Haiku

Acknowledgments

This book comes into existence because of many people's prayers. For that I have gratitude in my heart.

Writing poetry is a calling. I am thankful for the many strings of events that have allowed me to hear loud and clear my life's mission. I am humbled by the fact that I knew so little but was given so much. In the process of writing this book, one secret has been revealed to me: I don't need to understand all things, but I will be given answers when I ask. I don't need to know it all, but the entrance to truth is within me.

My deepest thanks go to my parents: Bernard Wang, a college principal and English professor, and my mother, Alice Wang-Chuang, a high school dean and Chinese teacher. Both my parents command highest respect in their professional lives but are devoted parents to their children. Both exemplify the way of wise parenting: let children develop their own strength while never losing faith in them. Both my parents practice the first virtue considered by all Chinese: filial piety toward their own parents. I am lucky to have two great role models to follow and, though I am full of shortcomings, have been blessed with their unconditional love.

Special thanks go to my beloved husband, Haidar. Without him, nothing would be possible. I decided to stay home with our two amazing children, Andrew and Amanda, after they were born, and they have since shown me my step backward was actually a step forward.

I am very grateful to have my sister, Ra Sha, to share my life's journey. She has been my angel and my best friend. My appreciations also go to my brother, Dr. Bernard, my sister-in-law, Jane, and my brother-in-law, John. They are kind and intelligent role models our world needs.

A bouquet of flowers goes to my friends worldwide for their loving support: Yuki, Katherine, Sophie, Phyllis and Roger, Amy, Mary, Kaori, Christine, Mon Jing, Jun, Gia, Arlene and Doyle, Julia, Jacquy, Rebecca, Nicki, Winnie, Theresa and Margaret; to Jill and Scarlet, the founders of WBW Book Club; and to the club's members: Maria, Joanne, Renee, Krista, Julie, and Jamie. Your reviews and feedback of *Garden Haiku* have proved invaluable to me.

My acknowledgment won't be complete without mentioning the English teachers that have taught me in the past and the Kindergarten teachers that are teaching my children today. To Professor Shu-Chuang Chiu, Dr. Stone, Dr. Yauo-Lin, Dr. Ma, Dr. Rosenthal, Dr. Weston, Dr. Sanchez: you have inspired me to be who I am today. To Mrs. Bonjorni, Mrs. Elia, Mrs. Simon, Mrs. Karen, Mrs. Michelle, Mrs. Kim, Mrs. Lindsay, Mrs. Zhoa, Mrs. Georgina, and Ms. Krista: your patience and talents have instilled a love for learning in our children.

In addition, I wish to thank Robert Kiyosaki of Rich Dad and Ruth Clawson, my financial coach, for helping me make what's in my brain a true asset. Deepest thanks also go to Nathan Magsig, the mayor of Clovis, CA, who supports *Baby Haiku* and its message of putting family first.

I am also greatly thankful to Mr. Stephen Mitchell, who generously grants us the permission to reprint passages from his superb translation of Lao Tzu's *Tao Te Ching*.

Finally, my appreciation goes to you, reader of *Garden Haiku*. We have the future of our children in our hands, while they have our future in their hands. I would like to complete my acknowledgment with you in my mind.

Thank you.

Preface

For everyone who picks up *Garden Haiku*, it is not merely chance. This book is written for you. The author may have drawn much of her inspirations from her life and, in particular, her two young children, but this book is inspired by the new generation of children whose brighter vision will bring about a greater tomorrow.

As parents, we notice how different our own children appear to be. For one thing, they seem not to care about man-made toys that cost parents huge amounts of money, but prefer sand and dirt. They insist on playing with toys in their own peculiar ways. They seem to love fruits and vegetables and won't pay attention to finely prepared cuisine.

The children of this new generation are masters of simplicity. As parents and guardians, our primary duty is to keep their lives simple, both spiritually and physically.

It is time adults cleanse their hearts and lead lives good enough to be models to their children. Energy needs to be directed to serve others rather than one's self. Action needs to be guided by forgiveness rather than fairness. Our children are here to let us see life again. Anger and struggle, confusion and self-doubt are all constructive because those emotions humble the jaded mind. We need to learn patience and stay calm when teaching our children about life's lessons. Respect our children and we will earn their respect. Never use violence against our children, so they will never resort to or accept violence as a way of solving their problems.

Garden Haiku: Raising Your Child with Ancient Wisdom is your personal guide to raising happy and resourceful children. While the author herself is far from being a perfect mom, she has learned important principles of achieving a higher love from writing these haiku.

Each haiku deals with an image first and a message second. The purpose of those eighty messages is to heighten awareness that, while we take raising our children seriously, we take our lives seriously as well. If we miss our children's growth, we miss our own growth. If we miss our children's lives, we miss our own. Because our children hold mankind's future in their hands, they deserve selfless devotion.

Many parents find themselves bombarded with worries about raising children. But those worries are caused by trying to give their children the wrong things. What do children really need?

You know the answer, and *Garden Haiku* helps you put those answers on paper.

Raise our children, one smile at a time.

Clovis, California, 2007

Author's Notes
on *Garden Haiku*

Haiku, by definition, is a form of Japanese poetry "that states in three lines of five, seven and five syllables a clear picture designed to arouse a distinct emotion and suggest a specific spiritual insight." (Holman and Harmon, *A Handbook to Literature*, 230).

Being aware of the differences in syllables between the Eastern and Western language systems, I have naturally focused on the spirit (Zen) rather than the form (seventeen syllables) of haiku. When a haiku appears in my mind, I spontaneously write it down. As Lao Tzu puts it, "true mastery can be gained/ by letting things go their own way. / It can't be gained by interfering." I decided to let the haiku remain the way they are rather than prune them to seventeen syllables. I also chose not to use periods on the third lines like some of my fellow haiku poets, mainly because it fits my style and also the original Japanese haiku do not use end punctuation.

The contents of *Garden Haiku* fall into four categories: messages for parents, messages for children, haiku on my children and family, and nature/season haiku. While *Garden Haiku* addresses parents and writes about young children, the book is meant for everyone. The themes and values are universal: we all grow from childhood to adulthood, and we are all our own best parents. We need to be a nurturing and assuring person who believes in ourselves and supports our dreams. The principles that we want to teach our children apply to our inner child, too. It is my aspiration that somewhere down the *Garden Haiku* path, the parental and poetic awareness will emerge and take effect in the hearts of the readers. Haiku may contain only three lines, but its voice can be traced back 2,500 years. We all come from a long line of history, and the frontier to a new history is right in front of us. Our children will also become ancestors soon, but the timeless wisdom from the ancients will always be within their reach if we help preserve it and inspire the next generation to carry on.

Lily Wang, 2007

Tao Te Ching[1]

Lao Tzu

10

Can you coax your mind from its wandering
And keep to the original oneness?
Can you let your body become
Supple as a newborn child's?
Can you cleanse your inner vision
Until you see nothing but the light?
Can you love people and lead them
Without imposing your will?
Can you deal with the most vital matters
By letting events take their course?
Can you step back from your own mind
And thus understand all things?
Giving birth and nourishing,
Having without possessing,
Acting with no expectations,
Leading and not trying to control:
This is the supreme virtue.

---

1 "The wisest book ever written," *Tao Te Ching* was written around 551 BC by Lao Tzu, an older contemporary of Confucius. Explaining the way of the universe, "it is the most widely translated book in world literature, next to the Bible" (Stephen Mitchell: *Tao Te Ching*, book cover).

41

....
Thus it is said:
The greatest art seems unsophisticated,
The greatest wisdom seems childish.

(Stephen Mitchell, translation)

Garden Haiku:
Raising Your Child
with Ancient Wisdom[2]

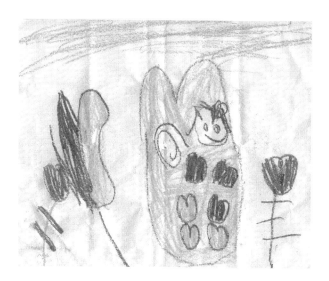

"I Love My Sister"
by Andrew Haddadin, 4 ½ years old.

---

2 *Garden Haiku* is a sequel to the author's first book, *Baby Haiku*. At the time of writing, the author's babies have grown into kindergartener and preschooler, ages five (Andrew) and three (Amanda).

I. Messages for Parents

1.

Garden

A seed a giant tree
A growth a connection
Children, parents' garden—

"Garden"
by Andrew Haddadin, 4 ½ years old.

2.

Life

Teach children
Not the limitation of ego
But omnipresence of Life—

3.

Angel[3]

Children can devil or angel be—
Put your hands on their backs
So they can feel their wings

---

3   A tribute to Dr. Doreen Virtue, author of more than twenty books, including *Divine Magic* and *The Crystal Children*.

4.

Sun

Children respond to
Warmth of the sun
Not force of the wind

5.

Storm

Discipline in a voice
Softer than a dropping pin—
Storm brings only destruction

6.

Stone

Disappointment is a heavy stone—
When a mistake is made,
Correct it; do not carry it

7.

Explore

Release the need to control—
Join the children's vision
To explore

8.

Television[4]

Creation cannot be confined in a box—
It is free,
When you explore with hands

---

4   A tribute to Marie Winn, author of *The Plug-In Drug*, a landmark study of television's negative impact on child development.

9.

Inner Eye

Open your third eye—
Do not run after paper,
When you have gold

10.

Lion

Bring the best in children—
Tame not the lion that rules the king
Ground not the eagle that soars the sky

11.

Turtle

Help children be who they are—
Stop not a fish that wants to swim
Push not a turtle by slow wins

12.

Magic Wand

Health is a magic wand
That brings colors to all scenes
And makes daily life a mind's dream

13.

Fire

Illness is a great teacher
That fortifies the soul
With touches of fire

14.

Patience

Patience is to
Have no expectations
But greater acceptance

15.

Tree

Tree grows in its own wisdom—
Do not overkill
With attention

16.

Wave

Parental anger is a wave
Forming in momentum,
Forever threatening—

17.

Knife

Anger is a knife
That cuts the connection
Between souls—

18.

Deep Breath

Anger is fire ready to devour
Take plenty of deep breaths
To blow it out—

19.

Fountain

A child is a fountain—
For the sound of water
Attend with care

20.

Heaven

Children seldom condemn—
Hence they are residents
Of heaven

21.

Lotus

Replace reprimand
With encouragement—
A choice, a lotus moment

22.

Lighthouse

A child is a lighthouse, full of love—
To get to it,
Paddle with patience

23.

Resources

Parents have two resources—
Inner wisdom
And observation

24.

Education[5]

Children born with same goodness,
They follow different directions
Influence of education—

---

5   A tribute to *Three Character Classic*, a book written in the thirteenth century that later became a classic of Chinese children's literature. With text arranged in three-character verse, it teaches young children the importance of learning, elements of Chinese history, and the basis of morality.

25.

Simplicity

When a child is born,
His whole being is fresh—
Nurture with simplicity

26.

Mirror

Children mirror
What's inside their parents
And more—

27.

Crown

A wreath of light
Is crowning every child
Do not break it with might—

28.

Soil

Fertilize children with soil
Of spiritual strength—
Material gifts spoil

29.

Moderation

The art of parenting is moderation—
Too much rain brings the flood
Too much sun dries the land

30.

Gardener

Parents are gardeners
With soul duty
To grow tender buds into full bloom

II. Messages for Children

31.

Unique

You are unique—
Through you
The world is born again

"Unique"
by Andrew Haddadin, 4 ½ years old.

32.

Temper

Children of temper listen to
Children with hunger—
You hold the power to save each other

33.

Respect[6]

Like a flower bows to the wind,
My child, lower your head
When life speaks its wisdom—

---

6   A tribute to *The Twenty-Four Filial Exemplars*, a traditional Chinese literature that teaches children love and respect for one's parents and ancestors.

34.

Mercy[7]

When the light of mercy dims—
Evil lurches
In despair of night

35.

Candle[8]

Burn your special gift
To keep the candle on—
A little light dissipates darkest night

---

8   A tribute to the great children's troubadour, Raffi, and his rendition of the traditional song "This Little Light of Mine" and other award-winning music.

36.

Forgiveness[9]

Forgiveness is the hardest thing—
It withstands the cross
And is superior to any weapon

---

9   A tribute to Jesus Christ.

37.

Grass

Like the grass raises its head
Each time it is pressed—
Persevere, till you surmount

38.

Tripod

Parents, teachers, and children
Tripod that sustains
Solid learning—

39.

Compassion

Child, be compassionate
Because everything is in you—
In origin, no division

40.

Courage

Innocence and courage—
What a child has now
What a child needs tomorrow

III. Haiku on My
Children and Family

.

41.

Rain

First day at school:
He cannot stop crying
The incessant April rain

42.

Fish

Second week at school:
He swims off stream
To join fish in the ocean

43.

Dancer[10]

My rejection is a cue
That sends my little dancer
Tip tapping with anger—

44.

Song[11]

"What is your name?" he chases—
The bird simply flies away
Leaving him a song

---

11   A tribute to Rabindranath Tagore (1861–1941), the Indian Nobel laureate, author of *The Flight of Birds* and *Gitanjali (song offerings)*.

45.

Mermaid

From the murmur of waves
Emerge several true words
My mermaid has found her tongue—

46.

Circus

A toddler's first steps—
The tightrope walker starts,
The circus holds its breath

47.

Peace

They have faces of angels
And the energy of nuclear bombs
In this New Age, we pray for peace—

48.

Crystals

She is made of chandelier—
When she cries,
Crystals are falling

49.

Sunbeam

Her face is a sun—
When she beams,
The smile reaches a thousand things

50.

Tank Engine[12]

He is a tank engine
That makes noises
Wherever he goes—

"Train"
by Andrew Haddadin, 4 ½ years old.

---

12 A tribute to the creator of Thomas the Tank Engine, Rev. W. Awdry. Awdry first made up stories of Thomas and his friends to amuse his three-year-old son, Christopher. More than twenty-five million of the books have sold in the United States and close to eighty million have sold worldwide.

51.

Cinderella[13]

Cinderella tries mom's shoes
Yours is the one
That the prince fits—

13   A tribute to the Brothers Grimm (1785–1863) and Charles Perrault (1628–1703), who helped preserve fairy tales and folklores so children today can experience the power of magic and imagination.

52.

Dolphin

In tranquil blue
She swims with freedom,
A peace-loving dolphin—

53.

Aphrodite[14]

She carries hues of beauty
In sleep, in anger, and in joy—
She is a miniature of Aphrodite

---

14 A tribute to Homer, the legendary Greek poet who lived in the seventh or eighth century BC and is credited with the authorship of *The Iliad* and *The Odyssey*. Aphrodite is the Greek goddess of love and beauty.

54.

Little Hero

He refuses rejection
And detests intimidation—
He is a hero of the little nation

55.

Butterfly Kisses

Her butterfly kisses,
So soft as silk touching my lips
I wish they had never left—

56.

Ballerina

She hums and rolls
Before bedtime—
Ballerina in a musical box

57.

Dimples

His smiling dimples,
Ripples on the lake
Ever widening—

58.

Grace

Moving shadows
Unaware of
Grace in every step—

59.

Sibling[15]

Siblings are hands and feet
Bonded with one soul—
Each plays an essential role

15   A tribute to *Siblings Without Rivalry* by Adele Faber and Elaine Mazlish.

60.
Reality

Babies give us dreams—
Preschoolers
Bring us reality

61.

Lessons

Did my greenness make you
Stumble for rhythm?
Imperfect world has perfect lessons—

62.

Handprints

Their handprints are
Maple leaves falling from the tree
Etched in my diary—

63.

Purity

My child, what purity!
Like the shore constantly cleanses itself
You are ready to forgive—

64.

Timber Lodge

Before Daddy, you are a tree, great and free
Now you become a timber lodge
Providing strength and security—

65.

Husbandry

The sweetest fruit on his tree
He saves for me—
Love in husbandry

66.

Grandchild

In you, I see your mom's yesterday
My lovely grandchild,
You make time return—

67.

Grandparents

Parental love and beyond—
Grandparents' embrace is
Life's full cycle arrived and begun

68.

Harmony

Every child brings a new energy
To the family
In search of harmony

69.

Snow Play

Where snow reaches sky,
Children in sleigh fly,
Happiness exudes from paradise—

70.

Well

Within every child is a well—
Fill it with love,
So it will feed them for life

IV. Nature/Season Haiku

71.

Spring

Butterflies caress our garden
Fruit trees in full bloom
Our personal spring

72.

Nature

Let children connect to nature—
Her river is their vein
Her abundance is their fortune

73.

Summer

When the summer heat
Becomes unbearable—
Keep a spring in your soul

74.

Roots

Entangled roots,
You go deeper into dirt
So treetop embraces the sky—

75.

Autumn

Mid-Autumn Festival[16]—
The moon is full
For this transitory world

16   The Mid-Autumn Festival is a popular Asian celebration of togetherness and abundance, dating back over 3,000 years to China's Zhou Dynasty. This holiday is also observed in Taiwan, Japan, Korea, Malasia, Singapore, and Vietnam.

76.

Flower

The fragility of a flower
Enhances
Its beauty—

77.

Wind

The flower has all the
Seeds it needs to flourish—
Simply be the wind

78.

Snow

The winter snow is children's purity—
Softly descending
Turning dust into feather

79.

Winter

In the coldest winter,
The bird still sings
For the spring she believes in—

80.

Plants

Children are plants
That thrive with water
Air and tender loving care—

"Heartland"
by Andrew Haddadin, 4 ½ years old.

The Greatest in
the Kingdom of Heaven

At that time the disciples came to Jesus, saying, "Who then is greatest in the kingdom of heaven?"

And Jesus called a little child to Him, set him in the midst of them, and said, "Assuredly I say to you, unless you change and become as little children, you will by no means enter the kingdom of heaven.

"Therefore whoever humbles himself as this little child is the greatest in the kingdom of heaven."

(Matthew 18:1-4)

References and Recommended Reading

On Haiku/Poetry

Blyth, R. H. *Haiku (4 volumes)*. Tokyo: Hokuseido Press, 1949.

Buxton, Richard. *The Complete World of Greek Mythology.* London: Thames & Hudson, 2004.

Hamill, Sam. *Crossing the Yellow River: Three Hundred Poems from the Chinese.* Rochester: BOA Editions, Ltd., 2000.

———. *The Sound of Water: Haiku by Basho, Buson, Issa, and Other Poets.* Boston: Shambhala, 1995.

Hass, Robert. *Essential Haiku Volume 20, Versions of Basho, Buson, & Issa.* Hopewell, N.J.: Ecco Press, 1995.

Holman, C. Hugh and Harmon, William. *A Handbook to Literature.* 5th ed. New York: Macmillan, 1986.

Kerouac, Jack. *Book of Haikus.* New York: Penguin, 2003.

Mitchell, Stephen. *Tao Te Ching.* New York: HarperCollins, 1988.

Tagore, Rabindranath. *Gitanjali (song offerings).* London: Macmillan, 1949.

Thoreau, Henry David. *Walden and Other Writings; Introduction by Ralph Waldo Emerson.* Ed. Atkinson, Brooks. New York: Modern Library, 2000.

Virtue, Doreen. *Divine Magic: A New Interpretation of the Classic Hermetic Manual The Kybalion.* Carlsbad: Hay House, 2006.

Washington, Peter. Ed. *Haiku.* New York: Knopff, 2003.

Wright, Richard. *Haiku, This Other World.* New York: Arcade Pub., 1998.

On Parenting

Biddulph, Steve. *Raising Boys: Why Boys Are Different—And How to Help Them Become Happy and Well-Balanced Men*. Berkeley: Celestial Arts, 1998.

Faber, Adele and Mazlish, Elaine. *How to Talk So Kids Will Listen & Listen So Kids Will Talk*. New York: Avon Books, 1980.

———. *Siblings Without Rivalry: How to Help Your Children Live Together So You Can Live Too*. New York: Avon Books, 1998.

Guo, Jujing. *The Twenty-four Filial Exemplars*. Taipei, Taiwan: Windmill Press, 1997.

Kiyosaki, Robert T. and Lechter, Sharon L. *Rich Dad's Rich Kid, Smart Kid: Giving Your Children a Financial Headstart*. New York: Warner Books, 2001.

Rosemond, John. *John Rosemond's Six-Point Plan for Raising Happy, Healthy Children*. Kansas City: Andrews and McMeel, 1989.

———. *Making The "Terrible" Twos Terrific*. Kansas City: Andrews and McMeel, 1993.

———. *Parent Power!* Kansas City: Andrews and McMeel, 1981.

Shelov, Steven P. Ed. *Caring for Your Baby and Young Child: Birth to Age 5*. New York: Bantam Books, 2004.

Turansky, Scott and Miller, Joanne. *Say Goodbye to Whining, Complaining, and Bad Attitudes ... in You and Your Kids*. Colorado Springs: WaterBrook Press, 2005.

Virtue, Doreen. *The Crystal Children*. Carlsbad: Hay House, 2003.

Wang, Yinglin. *Sanzi Jing: Three-Character Classic: A Confucian Roadmap for Kids*. Taipei, Taiwan: ACME Cultural Enterprise, 2004.

Winn, Marie. *The Plug-In Drug: Television, Computers, and Family Life.* New York: Penguin, 2002.

Recommended Reading for Young Children

Awdry, Rev. W. *Thomas the Tank Engine Story Collection.* London: Dean, 2002.

Baxter, Nicola. *Fairy Tales from the Brothers Grimm.* New York: Smithmark, 1997.

Brown, Margaret Wise. *Goodnight Moon.* New York: HarperCollins Publishers, 2005.

Carle, Eric. *The Very Hungry Caterpillar.* New York: Phiomel Books, 1994.

Crews, Nina. *The Neighborhood Mother Goose.* New York: Greenwillow Books, 2004.

Falconer, Ian. *Olivia.* New York: Atheneum Books for Young Readers, 2000.

Katz, Karen. *My First Chinese New Year.* New York: Henry Holt and Company, 2004.

Laan, Nancy Van. *When Winter Comes.* New York: Atheneum Books for Young Readers, 2000.

Leventhal, Debra. *What Is Your Language?* New York: Dutton Children's Books, 1994.

Mannis, Celeste. *One Leaf Rides the Wind: Counting in a Japanese Garden.* New York: Viking, 2002.

Martin, Bill Jr. and Archambault, John. *Chicka Chicka Boom Boom.* New York: Simon & Shuster, 1991.

Martin, David. *We've All Got Bellybuttons!* Cambridge, Mass.: Candlewick Press, 2005.

McKissack, Patricia C. *Ma Dear's Aprons.* New York: Atheneum Books for Young Readers, 1997.

Mollel, Tololwa M. *My Rows and Piles of Coins.* New York: Clarion Books, 1999.

Pan, Show Fan. Ed. *Tang Poems for Young Readers.* Taipei, Taiwan: ACME Cultural Enterprise, 2004.

Raffi. CDs including

Baby Beluga. Cambridge, Mass.: Rounder Records, 1996.

Everything grows. Cambridge, Mass.: Rounder Records, 1987.

One Light, One Sun. Willowdale, Ontario: A & M, 1985.

Rise and Shine. Cambridge, Mass., Rounder Records, 1982.

Raffi in Concert. Cambridge, Mass.: Rounder Records, 2002.

Singable Songs for the Very Young. Universal City, CA: MCA, 1976.

Simmons, Jane. *Come Along, Daisy!* Boston: Little, Brown, 2001.

Taback, Simms. *Joseph Had a Little Overcoat.* New York: Viking, 1999.

Index of Haiku
in Alphabetical Order

978-0-595-43095-6
0-595-43095-3

7002541R0

Made in the USA
Lexington, KY
11 October 2010